Proposed Amendments to the U.S. Constitution 1787-2001

IN FOUR VOLUMES

Supplement Volume IV
2001-2010

Proposed Amendments to the U.S. Constitution 1787-2001

John R. Vile, Editor

IN FOUR VOLUMES

Supplement Volume IV
2001-2010

THE LAWBOOK EXCHANGE, LTD.
Clark, New Jersey

ISBN 978-1-58477-225-5 (Set)
ISBN 978-1-61619-141-2 (Vol.I)
ISBN 978-1-61619-142-9 (Vol.II)
ISBN 978-1-61619-143-6 (Vol.III)
ISBN 978-1-61619-153-5 (Vol.IV Supplement)

Lawbook Exchange edition 2011

The Lawbook Exchange, Ltd.
33 Terminal Avenue
Clark, New Jersey 07066-1321

Please see our website for a selection of our other publications and fine facsimile reprints of classic works of legal history:
www.lawbookexchange.com

Library of Congress Cataloging-in-Publication Data

Proposed amendments to the U.S. Constitution: 1787-2001 / John R. Vile, editor.
p. cm.
Includes bibliographical references and index.
ISBN 1-58477-225-5 (cloth: alk. paper)
1. Constitutional amendments—United States. I. Title: Proposed amendments to the US
Constitution. II. Title: Proposed amendments to the United States Constitution.
III. Vile, John R.

KF4557 .P76 2002
342.73'035—dc2l 2002040563

Printed in the United States of America on acid-free paper

General Contents

Volume I

Introduction
Dr. John R. Vile **ix**

The Articles of Confederation **xix**

Constitution of the United States of America and its Amendments **xxix**

Dates Amendments to the U.S. Constitution Were Proposed and Ratified **li**

Constitution of the Confederate States of America **liii**

The Proposed Amendments to the Constitution of the United State During the First Century of Its History (1897)
Herman V. Ames **1**

Volume II

Proposed Amendments to the Constitution of the United States Introduced in Congress from December 4, 1889 to July 2, 1926, S. Doc. No. 93, 69th Cong. 1st Sess. (1926) **443**

Proposed Amendments to the Constitution, a Monograph on the Resolutions introduced in Congress Proposing Amendments to the Constitution of the United States of America, H. Doc. 551, 70th Cong., 2d Sess. (1929)
Michael Angelo Musmanno **595**

Proposed Amendments to the Constitution of the United States Introduced in Congress from the 69th Congress, 2d Session through the 87th Congress, 2d Session, December 6, 1926 to January 3, 1963, S. Doc. No. 163, 87th Cong. 2d Sess. (1963) **861**

Volume III

Proposed Amendments to the Constitution of the United States Introduced in Congress from the 88th Congress, 1st Session through the 90th Congress 2d Session, January 9, 1963 to January 3, 1969, S. Doc. No. 91-38, 91st Cong. 2d Sess. (1969) **1143**

Proposed Amendments to the Constitution of the United States Introduced in Congress from the 91st Congress, 1st Session through the 98th Congress, 2d Session, January 1969-December 1984, CSR Report No. 85-36 GOV
Richard Davis **1263**

Proposed Amendments to the Constitution: 99th-101st Congress (1985-1990)
Daryl B. Harris **1587**

Proposed Amendments to the United States Constitution, 102nd - first half of 107th Congresses (1991-2001) **1663**

Amendments Proposed by Two-Thirds Majorities of Congress but not Ratified by the States **1718**

List of Applicants by the States to Congress for a Constitutional Convention **1720**

Comprehensive Index of Proposed Amendments to the U.S. Constitution, 1787-2001 **1737**

About the Editor **1809**

Supplement Volume IV

Proposed Amendments to the United States Constitution, second half of 107th- 111th Congresses (2001-2010)

Introduction **xi**

107th Congress (2001-2002, Cont.) **13**

108 Congress (2003-2004) **17**

109th Congress (2005-2006) **33**

110th Congress (2007-2008) **47**

111th Congress (2009-2010) **59**

(Index continued from Vol. III, p. 1664)

Subject Index **73**

Sponsor Index **77**

Contents

Volume IV (Supplement 2001-2010)

Introduction xi

107th Congress (2001-2002, Cont.) 13
House....................692-707 (16)
Senate....................708-711 (4)
New Total for 107th Congress (77)

108 Congress (2003-2004) 17
House....................712-775 (64)
Senate....................776-789 (14)
Total for 108th Congress (78)

109th Congress (2005-2006) 33
House....................790-847 (58)
Senate....................848-861 (14)
Total for 109th Congress (72)

110th Congress (2007-2008) 47
House....................862-914 (53)
Senate....................915-926 (12)
Total for 110th Congress (65)

111th Congress (2009-2010) 59
House....................927-983 (54)
Senate....................984-1001 (18)
Total for 111th Congress (72)

(Index continued from Vol. III, p. 1664)
Subject Index 73
Sponsor Index 77

About The Editor 81

Introduction

This supplement updates the third volume of *Proposed Amendments to the U.S. Constitution, 1787-2001*, which the Lawbook Exchange first published in 2003 and which it is republishing with a more colorful cover. This supplement represents a continuing effort to track amendments that members of Congress have proposed throughout the history of the republic. Were this material to have been incorporated within Volume III, it would have begun on p. 1703.

The information in this supplement makes no pretense to originality. I have taken most of this material directly from the Library of Congress website. Because constitutional amendments require adoption by two-thirds majorities in both houses of Congress, members of Congress introduce most of these in the form of Joint Resolutions. Since these are not the only subject of such resolutions, I have weeded out those resolutions that did not deal with amendments. Thus, the H.J. and S.J numbers are not always consecutive.

I have otherwise left the materials in the form that I found them except for three particulars. First, I added the party affiliations of those who introduced each resolution, to correspond with information provided in the earlier volumes. Second, I deleted references to the committee to which each resolution was referred (almost invariably either the House or Senate Judiciary Committee) as well as most subsequent actions taken by that body. Third, I have added both a subject and a sponsor index to the proposals over the past ten years to facilitate further research.

The original three volumes tracked the number of amending proposals that members of Congress have introduced. Because the last volume of that work was published in the middle of the 107th Congress (2001-2002), this volume continues the numbering system used there. It ended on number 691, so this begins with 692. This number does not correspond to a number on the Library of Congress website but is added purely for indexing purposes.

As long as the Constitution is recognized as fundamental law, any proposed changes to this law will continue to be potentially consequential. This supplement, like the earlier three volumes, is largely a data base for scholars who wish to conduct further research in this area. Those who are interested in updated secondary commentary both on amendments that members of Congress have proposed and grander proposals for constitutional change that other individuals have authored might want to consult the third edition of my *Encyclopedia of Constitutional Amendments, Proposed Amendments, and Amending Issues, 1789-2010.*

John R. Vile,
Middle Tennessee State University

107th Congress (2001-2002)

Beginning from end of last volume.

House

692. H.J.RES.72
Proposing an amendment to the Constitution of the United States regarding the right to vote.
Sponsor: Rep Jackson, Jesse L., Jr. [D, IL-2] (introduced 11/6/2001)
Cosponsors (None)

693. H.J.RES.77
Proposing an amendment to the Constitution of the United States regarding the appointment of individuals to serve as Members of the House of Representatives when, in a national emergency, a significant number of Members are unable to serve.
Sponsor: Rep Lofgren, Zoe [D, CA-16] (introduced 12/5/2001)
Cosponsors (None)

694. H.J.RES.81
Proposing an amendment to the Constitution of the United States restoring religious freedom.
Sponsor: Rep Istook, Ernest J., Jr. [R, OK-5] (introduced 12/20/2001)
Cosponsors (88)

695. H.J.RES.85
Proposing an amendment to the Constitution to provide for a balanced budget for the United States Government and for greater accountability in the enactment of tax legislation.
Sponsor: Rep Berry, Marion [D, AR-1] (introduced 3/12/2002)
Cosponsors (17)

696. H.J.RES.86
Proposing a balanced budget amendment to the Constitution of the United States.
Sponsor: Rep Istook, Ernest J., Jr. [R, OK-5] (introduced 4/11/2002)
Cosponsors (127)

697. H.J.RES.88
Proposing an amendment to the Constitution of the United States to protect the rights of crime victims.
Sponsor: Rep Royce, Edward R. [R, CA-39] (introduced 4/23/2002)
Cosponsors (None)

698. H.J.RES.90
Proposing an amendment to the Constitution to provide for a balanced budget for the United States Government and for greater accountability in the enactment of tax legislation.
Sponsor: Rep Berry, Marion [D, AR-1] (introduced 4/25/2002)
Cosponsors (20)

699. H.J.RES.91
Proposing an amendment to the Constitution of the United States to protect the rights of crime victims.
Sponsor: Rep Chabot, Steve [R, OH-1] (introduced 5/2/2002)
Cosponsors (22)

700. H.J.RES.93
Proposing an amendment to the Constitution of the United States relating to marriage.
Sponsor: Rep Shows, Ronnie [D, MS-4] (introduced 5/15/2002)
Cosponsors (22)

701. H.J.RES.96
Proposing a tax limitation amendment to the Constitution of the United States.
Sponsor: Rep Sessions, Pete [R, TX-5] (introduced 6/6/2002)
Cosponsors (155)

702. H.J.RES.99
Proposing a spending limitation amendment to the Constitution of the United States.

Sponsor: Rep Smith, Nick [R, MI-7] (introduced 6/18/2002)
Cosponsors (None)

703. H.J.RES.102
Proposing an amendment to the Constitution of the United States to guarantee the right to recite the Pledge of Allegiance to the Flag.
Sponsor: Rep Pickering, Charles W. "Chip" [R, MS-3] (introduced 6/26/2002)
Cosponsors (13)

704. H.J.RES.103
Proposing an amendment to the Constitution of the United States with respect to the Pledge of Allegiance.
Sponsor: Rep Green, Gene [D, TX-29] (introduced 6/27/2002)
Cosponsors (None)

705. H.J.RES.104
Proposing an amendment to the Constitution of the United States to protect the Pledge of Allegiance.
Sponsor: Rep Lucas, Frank D. [R, OK-6] (introduced 6/27/2002)
Cosponsors (1)

706. H.J.RES.106
Proposing an amendment to the Constitution of the United States respecting real and virtual child pornography.
Sponsor: Rep Brown, Henry E., Jr. [R, SC-1] (introduced 7/17/2002)
Cosponsors (37)

707. H.J.RES.108
Proposing an amendment to the Constitution of the United States to guarantee the right to use and recite the Pledge of Allegiance to the Flag and the national motto.
Sponsor: Rep Pickering, Charles W. "Chip" [R, MS-3] (introduced 7/25/2002)
Cosponsors (25)

Senate

708. S.J.RES.33

A joint resolution proposing an amendment to the Constitution of the United States relating to contributions and expenditures intended to affect elections.

Sponsor: Sen Hollings, Ernest F. [D, SC] (introduced 3/4/2002)

Cosponsors (9)

709. S.J.RES.35

A joint resolution proposing an amendment to the Constitution of the United States to protect the rights of crime victims.

Sponsor: Sen Feinstein, Dianne [D, CA] (introduced 4/15/2002)

Cosponsors (28)

710. S.J.RES.39

A joint resolution proposing an amendment to the Constitution of the United States relative to the reference to God in the Pledge of Allegiance and on United States currency.

Sponsor: Sen Landrieu, Mary L. [D, LA] (introduced 6/26/2002)

Cosponsors (1)

711. S.J.RES.43

A joint resolution proposing an amendment to the Constitution of the United States to guarantee the right to use and recite the Pledge of Allegiance to the Flag and the national motto.

Sponsor: Sen Lott, Trent [R, MS] (introduced 8/1/2002)

Cosponsors (None)

108th Congress (2003-2004)

House

712. H.J.RES.4
Proposing an amendment to the Constitution of the United States authorizing the Congress to prohibit the physical desecration of the flag of the United States.
Sponsor: Rep Cunningham, Randy (Duke) [R, CA-50] (introduced 1/7/2003)
Cosponsors (213)

713. H.J.RES.5
Proposing an amendment to the Constitution of the United States to permit the Congress to limit expenditures in elections for Federal office.
Sponsor: Rep Dingell, John D. [D, MI-15] (introduced 1/7/2003)
Cosponsors (None)

714. H.J.RES.6
Proposing an amendment to the Constitution to provide for a balanced budget for the United States Government and for greater accountability in the enactment of tax legislation.
Sponsor: Rep Emerson, Jo Ann [R, MO-8] (introduced 1/7/2003)
Cosponsors (1)

715. H.J.RES.7
Proposing an amendment to the Constitution of the United States relating to voluntary school prayer.
Sponsor: Rep Emerson, Jo Ann [R, MO-8] (introduced 1/7/2003)
Cosponsors (1)

716. H.J.RES.8
Proposing an amendment to the Constitution of the United States

authorizing the Congress and the States to prohibit the act of desecration of the flag of the United States and to set criminal penalties for that act.
Sponsor: Rep Emerson, Jo Ann [R, MO-8] (introduced 1/7/2003)
Cosponsors (2)

717. H.J.RES.9
Proposing an amendment to the Constitution of the United States with respect to the right to life.
Sponsor: Rep Emerson, Jo Ann [R, MO-8] (introduced 1/7/2003)
Cosponsors (3)

718. H.J.RES.10
Proposing an amendment to the Constitution of the United States to protect the rights of crime victims.
Sponsor: Rep Royce, Edward R. [R, CA-40] (introduced 1/7/2003)
Cosponsors (2)

719. H.J.RES.11
Proposing an amendment to the Constitution of the United States to repeal the twenty-second article of amendment, thereby removing the limitation on the number of terms an individual may serve as President.
Sponsor: Rep Serrano, Jose E. [D, NY-16] (introduced 1/7/2003)
Cosponsors (3)

720. H.J.RES.14
Proposing an amendment to the Constitution of the United States to provide that Federal judges be reconfirmed by the Senate every 10 years.
Sponsor: Rep Hefley, Joel [R, CO-5] (introduced 1/27/2003)
Cosponsors (None)

721. H.J.RES.15
Proposing an amendment to the Constitution of the United States relative to abolishing personal income, estate, and gift taxes and prohibiting the United States Government from engaging in business in competition with its citizens.
Sponsor: Rep Paul, Ron [R, TX-14] (introduced 1/28/2003)
Cosponsors (2)

722. H.J.RES.16

Proposing an amendment to the Constitution of the United States to limit the number of consecutive terms that a Member of Congress may serve.
Sponsor: Rep Platts, Todd Russell [R, PA-19] (introduced 1/29/2003)
Cosponsors (None)

723. H.J.RES.21

Proposing an amendment to the Constitution of the United States regarding regulations on the amounts of expenditures of personal funds made by candidates for election for public office.
Sponsor: Rep Leach, James A. [R, IA-2] (introduced 2/5/2003)
Cosponsors (None)

724. H.J.RES.22

Proposing a balanced budget amendment to the Constitution of the United States.
Sponsor: Rep Istook, Ernest J., Jr. [R, OK-5] (introduced 2/13/2003)
Cosponsors (133)

725. H.J.RES.25

Proposing an amendment to the Constitution of the United States to repeal the 22nd amendment to the Constitution.
Sponsor: Rep Hoyer, Steny H. [D, MD-5] (introduced 2/25/2003)
Cosponsors (7)

726. H.J.RES.26

Proposing an amendment to the Constitution of the United States to protect the Pledge of Allegiance.
Sponsor: Rep Lucas, Frank D. [R, OK-3] (introduced 2/27/2003)
Cosponsors (2)

727. H.J.RES.28

Proposing an amendment to the Constitution of the United States regarding the right to vote.
Sponsor: Rep Jackson, Jesse L., Jr. [D, IL-2] (introduced 3/4/2003)
Cosponsors (45)

728. H.J.RES.29

Proposing an amendment to the Constitution of the United States regarding

the right of all citizens of the United States to a public education of equal high quality.
Sponsor: Rep Jackson, Jesse L., Jr. [D, IL-2] (introduced 3/4/2003)
Cosponsors (37)

729. H.J.RES.30
Proposing an amendment to the Constitution of the United States regarding the right of citizens of the United States to health care of equal high quality.
Sponsor: Rep Jackson, Jesse L., Jr. [D, IL-2] (introduced 3/4/2003)
Cosponsors (35)

730. H.J.RES.31
Proposing an amendment to the Constitution of the United States relating to equality of rights and reproductive rights.
Sponsor: Rep Jackson, Jesse L., Jr. [D, IL-2] (introduced 3/4/2003)
Cosponsors (5)

731. H.J.RES.32
Proposing an amendment to the Constitution of the United States respecting the right to decent, safe, sanitary, and affordable housing.
Sponsor: Rep Jackson, Jesse L., Jr. [D, IL-2] (introduced 3/4/2003)
Cosponsors (5)

732. H.J.RES.33
Proposing an amendment to the Constitution of the United States respecting the right to a clean, safe, and sustainable environment.
Sponsor: Rep Jackson, Jesse L., Jr. [D, IL-2] (introduced 3/4/2003)
Cosponsors (5)

733. H.J.RES.34
Proposing an amendment to the Constitution of the United States relative to taxing the people of the United States progressively.
Sponsor: Rep Jackson, Jesse L., Jr. [D, IL-2] (introduced 3/4/2003)
Cosponsors (5)

734. H.J.RES.35
Proposing an amendment to the Constitution of the United States respecting the right to full employment and balanced growth.

Sponsor: Rep Jackson, Jesse L., Jr. [D, IL-2] (introduced 3/4/2003)
Cosponsors (5)

735. H.J.RES.37

Proposing an amendment to the Constitution of the United States relative to equal rights for men and women.
Sponsor: Rep Maloney, Carolyn B. [D, NY-14] (introduced 3/12/2003)
Cosponsors (202)

736. H.J.RES.39

Proposing an amendment to the Constitution of the United States relative to references to God in the Pledge of Allegiance and on United States coins and currency.
Sponsor: Rep Carter, John R. [R, TX-31] (introduced 3/13/2003)
Cosponsors (None)

737. H.J.RES.40

Proposing an amendment to the Constitution of the United States to guarantee the right to use and recite the Pledge of Allegiance to the Flag and the national motto.
Sponsor: Rep Pickering, Charles W. "Chip" [R, MS-3] (introduced 3/18/2003)
Cosponsors (11)

738. H.J.RES.42

Proposing an amendment to the Constitution of the United States to deny United States citizenship to individuals born in the United States to parents who are neither United States citizens nor persons who owe permanent allegiance to the United States.
Sponsor: Rep Paul, Ron [R, TX-14] (introduced 3/20/2003)
Cosponsors (4)

739. H.J.RES.43

Proposing an amendment to the Constitution of the United States to limit the number of terms that a Member of Congress may serve.
Sponsor: Rep Vitter, David [R, LA-1] (introduced 3/26/2003)
Cosponsors (None)

740. H.J.RES.44

Proposing an amendment to the Constitution of the United States to provide

that no person born in the United States will be a United States citizen unless a parent is a United States citizen, or is lawfully admitted for permanent residence in the United States, at the time of the birth.
Sponsor: Rep Foley, Mark [R, FL-16] (introduced 3/31/2003)
Cosponsors (16)

741. H.J.RES.46
Proposing an amendment to the Constitution of the United States restoring religious freedom.
Sponsor: Rep Istook, Ernest J., Jr. [R, OK-5] (introduced 4/9/2003)
Cosponsors (103)

742. H.J.RES.47
Proposing an amendment to the Constitution of the United States respecting the right to a home.
Sponsor: Rep Rangel, Charles B. [D, NY-15] (introduced 4/9/2003)
Cosponsors (None)

743. H.J.RES.48
Proposing an amendment to the Constitution of the United States to protect the rights of crime victims.
Sponsor: Rep Chabot, Steve [R, OH-1] (introduced 4/10/2003)
Cosponsors (23)

744. H.J.RES.50
Proposing a tax limitation amendment to the Constitution of the United States.
Sponsor: Rep Sessions, Pete [R, TX-32] (introduced 4/10/2003)
Cosponsors (75)

745. H.J.RES.53
Proposing an amendment to the Constitution of the United States to require Members of Congress and the President to forfeit the compensation paid to them starting at the conclusion of each fiscal year until all of the general appropriations bills for the following fiscal year are enacted.
Sponsor: Rep Ose, Doug [R, CA-3] (introduced 4/12/2003)
Cosponsors (None)

746. H.J.RES.54

Proposing a tax limitation amendment to the Constitution of the United States.

Sponsor: Rep Ose, Doug [R, CA-3] (introduced 4/12/2003)

Cosponsors (None)

747. H.J.RES.55

Proposing an amendment to the Constitution of the United States to require that Federal district court judges be reconfirmed every ten years by the executive and legislative authorities of the State in which they serve.

Sponsor: Rep Culberson, John Abney [R, TX-7] (introduced 5/7/2003)

Cosponsors (None)

748. H.J.RES.56

Proposing an amendment to the Constitution of the United States relating to marriage.

Sponsor: Rep Musgrave, Marilyn N. [R, CO-4] (introduced 5/21/2003)

Cosponsors (131)

749. H.J.RES.59

Proposing an amendment to the Constitution of the United States to permit persons who are not natural-born citizens of the United States, but who have been citizens of the United States for at least 35 years, to be eligible to hold the offices of President and Vice President.

Sponsor: Rep Snyder, Vic [D, AR-2] (introduced 6/11/2003)

Cosponsors (6)

750. H.J.RES.60

Proposing an amendment to the Constitution of the United States to authorize the line item veto.

Sponsor: Rep Andrews, Robert E. [D, NJ-1] (introduced 6/16/2003)

Cosponsors (7)

751. H.J.RES.61

Proposing an amendment to the Constitution of the United States to abolish the Federal income tax.

Sponsor: Rep Johnson, Sam [R, TX-3] (introduced 6/24/2003)

Cosponsors (5)

752. H.J.RES.65

Proposing an amendment to the Constitution of the United States respecting real and virtual child pornography.

Sponsor: Rep Brown, Henry E., Jr. [R, SC-1] (introduced 7/18/2003)

Cosponsors (17)

753. H.J.RES.66

Proposing an amendment to the Constitution of the United States to provide for terms of office for Members of the House of Representatives.

Sponsor: Rep Stenholm, Charles W. [D, TX-17] (introduced 7/24/2003)

Cosponsors (2)

754. H.J.RES.67

Proposing an amendment to the Constitution of the United States to permit persons who are not natural-born citizens of the United States, but who have been citizens of the United States for at least 20 years, to be eligible to hold the Office of President.

Sponsor: Rep Conyers, John, Jr. [D, MI-14] (introduced 9/3/2003)

Cosponsors (1)

755. H.J.RES.68

Proposing an amendment to the Constitution of the United States relating to school prayer.

Sponsor: Rep Murtha, John P. [D, PA-12] (introduced 9/17/2003)

Cosponsors (None)

756. H.J.RES.71

Proposing an amendment to the Constitution of the United States deeming Presidential nominees to be appointed at the time of nomination subject to disapproval by the Senate within 120 days of receiving the nomination from the President.

Sponsor: Rep McCotter, Thaddeus G. [R, MI-11] (introduced 10/1/2003)

Cosponsors (9)

757. H.J.RES.77

Proposing an amendment to the Constitution of the United States regarding the appointment of individuals to fill vacancies in the House of Representatives.

Sponsor: Rep Baird, Brian [D, WA-3] (introduced 11/19/2003)
Cosponsors (None)

758. H.J.RES.81
Proposing an amendment to the Constitution of the United States limiting the number of consecutive terms that a Senator or Representative may serve and providing for 4-year terms for Representatives.
Sponsor: Rep Owens, Major R. [D, NY-11] (introduced 11/21/2003)
Cosponsors (None)

759. H.J.RES.83
Proposing an amendment to the Constitution of the United States regarding the appointment of individuals to fill vacancies in the House of Representatives.
Sponsor: Rep Baird, Brian [D, WA-3] (introduced 12/8/2003)
Cosponsors (2)

760. H.J.RES.85
Proposing an amendment to the Constitution of the United States relating to the maintenance of a system of social insurance that provides Social Security for its citizens.
Sponsor: Rep Michaud, Michael H. [D, ME-2] (introduced 1/20/2004)
Cosponsors (None)

761. H.J.RES.86
Proposing a balanced budget amendment to the Constitution of the United States.
Sponsor: Rep Jenkins, William L. [R, TN-1] (introduced 1/21/2004)
Cosponsors (None)

762. H.J.RES.88
Proposing an amendment to the Constitution of the United States to provide that certain trust funds are outside the budget of the United States.
Sponsor: Rep Taylor, Gene [D, MS-4] (introduced 1/28/2004)
Cosponsors (7)

763. H.J.RES.89
Proposing an amendment to the Constitution of the United States regarding the appointment of individuals to fill vacancies in the House of

Representatives.
Sponsor: Rep Larson, John B. [D, CT-1] (introduced 3/11/2004)
Cosponsors (None)

764. H.J.RES.90
Proposing an amendment to the Constitution of the United States regarding the appointment of individuals to serve as Members of the House of Representatives when, in a national emergency, a significant number of Members are unable to serve.
Sponsor: Rep Lofgren, Zoe [D, CA-16] (introduced 3/11/2004)
Cosponsors (None)

765. H.J.RES.92
Proposing an amendment to the Constitution of the United States relating to Congressional succession.
Sponsor: Rep Rohrabacher, Dana [R, CA-46] (introduced 4/2/2004)
Cosponsors (None)

766. H.J.RES.94
Proposing an amendment to the Constitution of the United States to establish English as the official language of the United States.
Sponsor: Rep Goode, Virgil H., Jr. [R, VA-5] (introduced 4/29/2004)
Cosponsors (12)

767. H.J.RES.96
Proposing an amendment to the Constitution of the United States regarding the appointment of individuals to serve as Members of the House of Representatives when, in a national emergency, a significant number of Members are unable to serve due to death, resignation, or incapacity.
Sponsor: Rep Lofgren, Zoe [D, CA-16] (introduced 5/4/2004)
Cosponsors (None)

768. H.J.RES.101
Proposing an amendment to the Constitution of the United States regarding presidential election voting rights for residents of all United States territories and commonwealths.
Sponsor: Rep Christensen, Donna M. [D, VI] (introduced 7/22/2004)
Cosponsors (2)

769. H.J.RES.103
Every Vote Counts Amendment
Sponsor: Rep Green, Gene [D, TX-29] (introduced 9/14/2004)
Cosponsors (9)

770. H.J.RES.104
Proposing an amendment to the Constitution of the United States to make eligible for the Office of President a person who is not a natural born citizen of the United States but has been a United States citizen for at least 20 years.
Sponsor: Rep Rohrabacher, Dana [R, CA-46] (introduced 9/15/2004)
Cosponsors (None)

771. H.J.RES.105
Proposing an amendment to the Constitution of the United States to lower the age qualification for Senators from 30 years of age to 21 years of age and for Members of the House of Representatives from 25 years of age to 21 years of age.
Sponsor: Rep English, Phil [R, PA-3] (introduced 9/15/2004)
Cosponsors (None)

772. H.J.RES.106
Proposing an amendment to the Constitution of the United States relating to marriage.
Sponsor: Rep Musgrave, Marilyn N. [R, CO-4] (introduced 9/23/2004)
Cosponsors (121)

773. H.J.RES.109
Proposing an amendment to the Constitution of the United States to provide for the direct election of the President and Vice President by the popular vote of all citizens of the United States regardless of place of residence.
Sponsor: Rep Jackson, Jesse L., Jr. [D, IL-2] (introduced 10/8/2004)
Cosponsors (6)

774. H.J.RES.112
Proposing an amendment to the Constitution of the United States to abolish the Electoral College and to provide for the direct election of the President and Vice President of the United States.
Sponsor: Rep Lofgren, Zoe [D, CA-16] (introduced 11/18/2004)
Cosponsors (None)

775. H.J.RES.113

Proposing an amendment to the Constitution of the United States relating to the process by which the House of Representatives chooses the President of the United States in the event no candidate receives a majority of the electoral votes.

Sponsor: Rep Sherman, Brad [D, CA-27] (introduced 11/18/2004)

Cosponsors (None)

Senate

776. S.J.RES.1
A joint resolution proposing an amendment to the Constitution of the United States to protect the rights of crime victims.
Sponsor: Sen Kyl, Jon [R, AZ] (introduced 1/7/2003)
Cosponsors (26)

777. S.J.RES.2
A joint resolution proposing an amendment to the Constitution of the United States to require a balanced budget and protect Social Security surpluses.
Sponsor: Sen Craig, Larry E. [R, ID] (introduced 1/7/2003)
Cosponsors (1)

778. S.J.RES.4
A joint resolution proposing an amendment to the Constitution of the United States authorizing Congress to prohibit the physical desecration of the flag of the United States.
Sponsor: Sen Hatch, Orrin G. [R, UT] (introduced 1/16/2003)
Cosponsors (56)

779. S.J.RES.5
A joint resolution proposing an amendment to the Constitution of the United States relating to contributions and expenditures intended to affect elections.
Sponsor: Sen Hollings, Ernest F. [D, SC] (introduced 1/23/2003)
Cosponsors (1)

780. S.J.RES.7
A joint resolution proposing an amendment to the Constitution of the United States relative to the reference to God in the Pledge of Allegiance and on United States currency.
Sponsor: Sen Landrieu, Mary L. [D, LA] (introduced 3/3/2003)
Cosponsors (3)

781. S.J.RES.11
A joint resolution proposing an amendment to the Constitution of the United States relative to equal rights for women and men.
Sponsor: Sen Kennedy, Edward M. [D, MA] (introduced 3/18/2003)
Cosponsors (21)

S.J.RES.15
A joint resolution proposing an amendment to the Constitution of the United States to make eligible for the Office of President a person who has been a United States citizen for 20 years.
Sponsor: Sen Hatch, Orrin G. [R, UT] (introduced 7/10/2003)
Cosponsors (None)

783. S.J.RES.23
A joint resolution proposing an amendment to the Constitution of the United States providing for the event that one-fourth of the members of either the House of Representatives or the Senate are killed or incapacitated.
Sponsor: Sen Cornyn, John [R, TX] (introduced 11/5/2003)
Cosponsors (1)

784. S.J.RES.25
A joint resolution proposing an amendment to the Constitution of the United States relative to the line item veto.
Sponsor: Sen Dole, Elizabeth [R, NC] (introduced 11/19/2003)
Cosponsors (None)

785. S.J.RES.26
A joint resolution proposing an amendment to the Constitution of the United States relating to marriage.
Sponsor: Sen Allard, Wayne [R, CO] (introduced 11/25/2003)
Cosponsors (10)

786. S.J.RES.29
A joint resolution proposing an amendment to the Constitution of the United States which requires (except during time of war and subject to suspension by the Congress) that the total amount of money expended by the United States during any fiscal year not exceed the amount of certain revenue received by the United States during such fiscal year and not exceed 20 per centum of the gross national product of the United States during the previous calendar year.
Sponsor: Sen Shelby, Richard C. [R, AL] (introduced 3/11/2004)
Cosponsors (None)

787. S.J.RES.30
Marriage resolution [Federal Marriage Amendment: one man and one woman.]

Sponsor: Sen Allard, Wayne [R, CO] (introduced 3/22/2004)
Cosponsors (16)

788. S.J.RES.35
A joint resolution to repeal the seventeenth article of amendment to the Constitution of the United States.
Sponsor: Sen Miller, Zell [D, GA] (introduced 4/28/2004)
Cosponsors (None)

789. S.J.RES.40
Federal Marriage Amendment
Sponsor: Sen Allard, Wayne [R, CO] (introduced 7/7/2004)
Cosponsors (19)

109th Congress (2005-2006)

House

790. H.J.RES.1
Proposing an amendment to the Constitution of the United States regarding presidential election voting rights for residents of all United States territories and commonwealths.
Sponsor: Rep Christensen, Donna M. [D, VI] (introduced 1/4/2005)
Cosponsors (1)

791. H.J.RES.2
Proposing an amendment to the Constitution of the United States to permit persons who are not natural-born citizens of the United States, but who have been citizens of the United States for at least 20 years, to be eligible to hold the Office of President.
Sponsor: Rep Conyers, John, Jr. [D, MI-14] (introduced 1/4/2005)
Cosponsors (1)

792. H.J.RES.4
Proposing an amendment to the Constitution of the United States with respect to the right to life.
Sponsor: Rep Emerson, Jo Ann [R, MO-8] (introduced 1/4/2005)
Cosponsors (None)

793. H.J.RES.5
Proposing an amendment to the Constitution of the United States authorizing the Congress and the States to prohibit the act of desecration of the flag of the United States and to set criminal penalties for that act.
Sponsor: Rep Emerson, Jo Ann [R, MO-8] (introduced 1/4/2005)
Cosponsors (1)

794. H.J.RES.6

Proposing an amendment to the Constitution to provide for a balanced budget for the United States Government and for greater accountability in the enactment of tax legislation.

Sponsor: Rep Emerson, Jo Ann [R, MO-8] (introduced 1/4/2005)

Cosponsors (2)

795. H.J.RES.7

Proposing an amendment to the Constitution of the United States relating to voluntary school prayer.

Sponsor: Rep Emerson, Jo Ann [R, MO-8] (introduced 1/4/2005)

Cosponsors (1)

796. H.J.RES.8

Every Vote Counts Amendment

Sponsor: Rep Green, Gene [D, TX-29] (introduced 1/4/2005)

Cosponsors (2)

797. H.J.RES.9

Proposing an amendment to the Constitution of the United States to repeal the twenty-second article of amendment, thereby removing the limitation on the number of terms an individual may serve as President.

Sponsor: Rep Serrano, Jose E. [D, NY-16] (introduced 1/4/2005)

Cosponsors (None)

798. H.J.RES.10

Proposing an amendment to the Constitution of the United States authorizing the Congress to prohibit the physical desecration of the flag of the United States.

Sponsor: Rep Cunningham, Randy (Duke) [R, CA-50] (introduced 1/25/2005

Cosponsors (196)

799. H.J.RES.11

Proposing an amendment to the Constitution of the United States to limit the number of consecutive terms that a Member of Congress may serve.

Sponsor: Rep Platts, Todd Russell [R, PA-19] (introduced 1/25/2005)

Cosponsors (None)

800. H.J.RES.13

Proposing an amendment to the Constitution of the United States regarding regulations on the amounts of expenditures of personal funds made by candidates for election for public office.

Sponsor: Rep Leach, James A. [R, IA-2] (introduced 1/26/2005)

Cosponsors (None)

801. H.J.RES.14

Proposing an amendment to the Constitution of the United States relative to abolishing personal income, estate, and gift taxes and prohibiting the United States Government from engaging in business in competition with its citizens.

Sponsor: Rep Paul, Ron [R, TX-14] (introduced 1/26/2005)

Cosponsors (2)

802. H.J.RES.15

Proposing an amendment to the Constitution of the United States to make eligible for the Office of President a person who is not a natural born citizen of the United States but has been a United States citizen for at least 20 years.

Sponsor: Rep Rohrabacher, Dana [R, CA-46] (introduced 2/1/2005)

Cosponsors (None)

803. H.J.RES.16

Proposing an amendment to the Constitution of the United States to repeal the sixteenth article of amendment.

Sponsor: Rep King, Steve [R, IA-5] (introduced 2/1/2005)

Cosponsors (14)

804. H.J.RES.17

Proposing an amendment to the Constitution of the United States to provide for the direct election of the President and Vice President by the popular vote of the citizens of the United States.

Sponsor: Rep Engel, Eliot L. [D, NY-17] (introduced 2/9/2005)

Cosponsors (4)

805. H.J.RES.21

Proposing an amendment to the Constitution of the United States relating to school prayer.

Sponsor: Rep Murtha, John P. [D, PA-12] (introduced 2/16/2005)

Cosponsors (None)

806. H.J.RES.22
Proposing a balanced budget amendment to the Constitution of the United States.
Sponsor: Rep Cooper, Jim [D, TN-5] (introduced 2/17/2005)
Cosponsors (30)

807. H.J.RES.24
Proposing an amendment to the Constitution of the United States to repeal the 22nd amendment to the Constitution.
Sponsor: Rep Hoyer, Steny H. [D, MD-5] (introduced 2/17/2005)
Cosponsors (4)

808. H.J.RES.25
Proposing an amendment to the Constitution of the United States relating to the maintenance of a system of social insurance that provides social security for its citizens.
Sponsor: Rep Michaud, Michael H. [D, ME-2] (introduced 2/17/2005)
Cosponsors (None)

809. H.J.RES.26
Proposing an amendment to the Constitution of the United States relating to Congressional succession.
Sponsor: Rep Rohrabacher, Dana [R, CA-46] (introduced 2/17/2005)
Cosponsors (1)

810. H.J.RES.28
Proposing an amendment to the Constitution of the United States regarding the right to vote.
Sponsor: Rep Jackson, Jesse L., Jr. [D, IL-2] (introduced 3/2/2005)
Cosponsors (61)

811. H.J.RES.29
Proposing an amendment to the Constitution of the United States regarding the right of all citizens of the United States to a public education of equal high quality.

Sponsor: Rep Jackson, Jesse L., Jr. [D, IL-2] (introduced 3/2/2005)
Cosponsors (35)

812. H.J.RES.30

Proposing an amendment to the Constitution of the United States regarding he right of citizens of the United States to health care of equal high quality.

Sponsor: Rep Jackson, Jesse L., Jr. [D, IL-2] (introduced 3/2/2005)

Cosponsors (35)

813. H.J.RES.31

Proposing an amendment to the Constitution of the United States relating to equality of rights and reproductive rights.

Sponsor: Rep Jackson, Jesse L., Jr. [D, IL-2] (introduced 3/2/2005)

Cosponsors (None)

814. H.J.RES.32

Proposing an amendment to the Constitution of the United States respecting the right to decent, safe, sanitary, and affordable housing.

Sponsor: Rep Jackson, Jesse L., Jr. [D, IL-2] (introduced 3/2/2005)

Cosponsors (None)

815. H.J.RES.33

Proposing an amendment to the Constitution of the United States respecting the right to a clean, safe, and sustainable environment.

Sponsor: Rep Jackson, Jesse L., Jr. [D, IL-2] (introduced 3/2/2005)

Cosponsors (None)

816. H.J.RES.34

Proposing an amendment to the Constitution of the United States relative to taxing the people of the United States progressively.

Sponsor: Rep Jackson, Jesse L., Jr. [D, IL-2] (introduced 3/2/2005)

Cosponsors (None)

817. H.J.RES.35

Proposing an amendment to the Constitution of the United States respecting the right to full employment and balanced growth.

Sponsor: Rep Jackson, Jesse L., Jr. [D, IL-2] (introduced 3/2/2005)

Cosponsors (None)

818. H.J.RES.36

Proposing an amendment to the Constitution of the United States to abolish the Electoral College and provide for the direct election of the President

and Vice President by the popular vote of all citizens of the United States regardless of place of residence.
Sponsor: Rep Jackson, Jesse L., Jr. [D, IL-2] (introduced 3/2/2005)
Cosponsors (3)

819. H.J.RES.37
Proposing an amendment to the Constitution of the United States relative to equal rights for men and women.
Sponsor: Rep Maloney, Carolyn B. [D, NY-14] (introduced 3/15/2005)
Cosponsors (185)

820. H.J.RES.39
Proposing an amendment to the Constitution of the United States relating to marriage.
Sponsor: Rep Lungren, Daniel E. [R, CA-3] (introduced 3/17/2005)
Cosponsors (29)

821. H.J.RES.40
Proposing an amendment to the Constitution of the United States respecting the right to a home.
Sponsor: Rep Rangel, Charles B. [D, NY-15] (introduced 4/5/2005)
Cosponsors (None)

822. H.J.RES.41
Proposing an amendment to the Constitution of the United States to provide that no person born in the United States will be a United States citizen unless a parent is a United States citizen, or is lawfully admitted for permanent residence in the United States, at the time of the birth.
Sponsor: Rep Foley, Mark [R, FL-16] (introduced 4/13/2005)
Cosponsors (3)

823. H.J.RES.42
Proposing an amendment to the Constitution of the United States to permit persons who are not natural-born citizens of the United States, but who have been citizens of the United States for at least 35 years, to be eligible to hold the offices of President and Vice President.
Sponsor: Rep Snyder, Vic [D, AR-2] (introduced 4/14/2005)
Cosponsors (1)

824. H.J.RES.43

Proposing an amendment to the Constitution of the United States to establish English as the official language of the United States.

Sponsor: Rep Tancredo, Thomas G. [R, CO-6] (introduced 4/21/2005)

Cosponsors (4)

825. H.J.RES.46

Proposing an amendment to the Constitution of the United States to deny United States citizenship to individuals born in the United States to parents who are neither United States citizens nor persons who owe permanent allegiance to the United States.

Sponsor: Rep Paul, Ron [R, TX-14] (introduced 4/28/2005)

Cosponsors (4)

826. H.J.RES.49

Proposing an amendment to the Constitution of the United States regarding the appointment of individuals to serve as Members of the House of Representatives when, in a national emergency, a significant number of Members are unable to serve due to death, resignation, or incapacity.

Sponsor: Rep Lofgren, Zoe [D, CA-16] (introduced 5/12/2005)

Cosponsors (None)

827. H.J.RES.50

Proposing an amendment to the Constitution of the United States to abolish the Electoral College and to provide for the direct election of the President and Vice President of the United States.

Sponsor: Rep Lofgren, Zoe [D, CA-16] (introduced 5/12/2005)

Cosponsors (4)

828. H.J.RES.51

Proposing an amendment to the Constitution of the United States to allow debate to be closed on any measure, motion, or other matter pending before the Senate only by unanimous consent or the concurrence of three-fifths of the Senators.

Sponsor: Rep Pallone, Frank, Jr. [D, NJ-6] (introduced 5/23/2005)

Cosponsors (None)

829. H.J.RES.53

Proposing an amendment to the Constitution of the United States to provide

that Representatives shall be apportioned among the several States according to their respective numbers, counting the number of persons in each State who are citizens of the United States.
Sponsor: Rep Miller, Candice S. [R, MI-10] (introduced 6/9/2005)
Cosponsors (37)

830. H.J.RES.57
Proposing an amendment to the Constitution of the United States protecting religious freedom.
Sponsor: Rep Istook, Ernest J., Jr. [R, OK-5] (introduced 6/30/2005)
Cosponsors (116)

831. H.J.RES.58
Proposing a balanced budget amendment the Constitution of the United States.
Sponsor: Rep Istook, Ernest J., Jr. [R, OK-5] (introduced 7/13/2005)
Cosponsors (143)

832. H.J.RES.60
Proposing an amendment to the Constitution of the United States relating to the permissible uses for which private property may be taken.
Sponsor: Rep Aderholt, Robert B. [R, AL-4] (introduced 7/14/2005)
Cosponsors (7)

833. H.J.RES.62
Proposing an amendment to the Constitution of the United States to require that Federal district court judges be reconfirmed every ten years by the executive and legislative authorities of the State in which they serve.
Sponsor: Rep Culberson, John Abney [R, TX-7] (introduced 7/28/2005)
Cosponsors (15)

834. H.J.RES.63
Proposing an amendment to the Constitution of the United States to allow an item veto of appropriation bills.
Sponsor: Rep Kennedy, Mark R. [R, MN-6] (introduced 7/29/2005)
Cosponsors (1)

835. H.J.RES.67
Proposing an amendment to the Constitution of the United States to

authorize the line item veto.
Sponsor: Rep Platts, Todd Russell [R, PA-19] (introduced 9/21/2005)
Cosponsors (8)

836. H.J.RES.71

Proposing an amendment to the Constitution of the United States to authorize the President to reduce or disapprove any appropriation in any bill presented by Congress.
Sponsor: Rep Kennedy, Mark R. [R, MN-6] (introduced 11/4/2005)
Cosponsors (17)

837. H.J.RES.74

Proposing a balanced budget amendment to the Constitution of the United States.
Sponsor: Rep Jenkins, William L. [R, TN-1] (introduced 12/14/2005)
Cosponsors (None)

838. H.J.RES.76

Proposing an amendment to the Constitution of the United States relating to limitations on the amounts of contributions and expenditures that may be made in connection with campaigns for election to public office.
Sponsor: Rep Kaptur, Marcy [D, OH-9] (introduced 2/1/2006)
Cosponsors (None)

839. H.J.RES.77

Proposing an amendment to the Constitution of the United States to authorize the President to reduce or disapprove any appropriation or authorization of new direct spending in any bill presented by Congress.
Sponsor: Rep Stearns, Cliff [R, FL-6] (introduced 2/8/2006)
Cosponsors (None)

840. H.J.RES.80

Proposing an amendment the Constitution of the United States limiting the number of consecutive terms that a Senator or Representative may serve and providing for 4-year terms for Representatives.
Sponsor: Rep Owens, Major R. [D, NY-11] (introduced 3/2/2006)
Cosponsors (None)

841. H.J.RES.84
No Taxation Without Representation Amendment
Sponsor: Rep Akin, W. Todd [R, MO-2] (introduced 4/27/2006)
Cosponsors (3)

842. H.J.RES.85
Proposing an amendment to the Constitution of the United States to clarify that the Constitution neither prohibits voluntary prayer nor requires prayer in schools.
Sponsor: Rep Rahall, Nick J., II [D, WV-3] (introduced 5/4/2006)
Cosponsors (1)

843. H.J.RES.88
Marriage Protection Amendment
Sponsor: Rep Musgrave, Marilyn N. [R, CO-4] (introduced 6/6/2006)
Cosponsors (134)

844. H.J.RES.91
Proposing an amendment to the Constitution of the United States relating to marriage.
Sponsor: Rep Gohmert, Louie [R, TX-1] (introduced 7/11/2006)
Cosponsors (None)

845. H.J.RES.92
Proposing an amendment to the Constitution of the United States to ensure a free and adequate education for every child who is a citizen.
Sponsor: Rep Owens, Major R. [D, NY-11] (introduced 7/20/2006)
Cosponsors (None)

846. H.J.RES.98
Proposing a balanced budget amendment to the Constitution of the United States.
Sponsor: Rep Musgrave, Marilyn N. [R, CO-4] (introduced 9/28/2006)
Cosponsors (None)

847. H.J.RES.99
Health Protection Amendment
Sponsor: Rep McCollum, Betty [D, MN-4] (introduced 9/29/2006)
Cosponsors (None)

Senate

848. S.J.RES.1

Marriage Protection Amendment

Sponsor: Sen Allard, Wayne [R, CO] (introduced 1/24/2005)

Cosponsors (32)

849. S.J.RES.2

A joint resolution proposing an amendment to the Constitution of the United States relative to require a balanced budget and protect Social Security surpluses.

Sponsor: Sen Craig, Larry E. [R, ID] (introduced 1/24/2005)

Cosponsors (1)

850. S.J.RES.3

A joint resolution proposing an amendment to the Constitution of the United States relative to limiting the number of terms that a Member of Congress may serve.

Sponsor: Sen Vitter, David [R, LA] (introduced 2/10/2005)

Cosponsors (None)

851. S.J.RES.6

A joint resolution proposing an amendment to the Constitution of the United States to ensure continuity of congressional operations and the avoidance of martial law in the event of mass incapacitations or death in either House of Congress.

Sponsor: Sen Cornyn, John [R, TX] (introduced 2/17/2005)

Cosponsors (1)

852. S.J.RES.7

A joint resolution proposing an amendment to the Constitution of the United States relative to equal rights for men and women.

Sponsor: Sen Kennedy, Edward M. [D, MA] (introduced 3/15/2005)

Cosponsors (20)

853. S.J.RES.10

A joint resolution proposing an amendment to the Constitution of the United States which requires (except during time of war and subject to suspension

by Congress) that the total amount of money expended by the United States during any fiscal year not exceed the amount of certain revenue received by the United States during such fiscal year and not exceed 20 per centum of the gross national product of the United States during the previous calendar year.
Sponsor: Sen Shelby, Richard C. [R, AL] (introduced 3/16/2005)
Cosponsors (1)

854. S.J.RES.11
A joint resolution proposing an amendment to the Constitution of the United States to abolish the electoral college and to provide for the direct popular election of the President and Vice President of the United States.
Sponsor: Sen Feinstein, Dianne [D, CA] (introduced 3/16/2005)
Cosponsors (1)

856. S.J.RES.12
A joint resolution proposing an amendment to the Constitution of the United States authorizing Congress to prohibit the physical desecration of the flag of the United States.
Sponsor: Sen Hatch, Orrin G. [R, UT] (introduced 4/14/2005)
Cosponsors (59)
[Note: A vote on this measure narrowly failed in the Senate on 6/27/2006 by a vote of 66 – 34.]

856. S.J.RES.13
A joint resolution proposing an amendment to the Constitution of the United States relative to marriage.
Sponsor: Sen Brownback, Sam [R, KS] (introduced 4/14/2005)
Cosponsors (1)

857. S.J.RES.24
A joint resolution proposing an amendment to the Constitution of the United States relative to the reference to God in the Pledge of Allegiance and on United States currency.
Sponsor: Sen Landrieu, Mary L. [D, LA] (introduced 9/14/2005)
Cosponsors (None)

858. S.J.RES.25

A joint resolution proposing an amendment to the Constitution of the United States to authorize the President to reduce or disapprove any appropriation in any bill presented by Congress.

Sponsor: Sen Talent, Jim [R, MO] (introduced 9/27/2005)

Cosponsors (11)

859. S.J.RES.26

A joint resolution proposing an amendment to the Constitution of the United States relative to the line item veto.

Sponsor: Sen Dole, Elizabeth [R, NC] (introduced 9/27/2005)

Cosponsors (None)

860. S.J.RES.31

A joint resolution proposing an amendment to the Constitution of the United States relative to require a balancing of the budget.

Sponsor: Sen Allen, George [R, VA] (introduced 2/15/2006)

Cosponsors (None)

861. S.J.RES.35

A joint resolution proposing an amendment to the Constitution of the United States to clarify that the Constitution neither prohibits voluntary prayer nor requires prayer in schools.

Sponsor: Sen Byrd, Robert C. [D, WV] (introduced 4/27/2006)

Cosponsors (6)

110th Congress (2007-2008)

House

862. H.J.RES.1
Proposing a balanced budget amendment to the Constitution of the United States.
Sponsor: Rep Goodlatte, Bob [R, VA-6] (introduced 1/4/2007)
Cosponsors (163)

863. H.J.RES.2
Proposing an amendment the Constitution of the United States regarding presidential election voting rights for residents of all United States territories and commonwealths.
Sponsor: Rep Christensen, Donna M. [D, VI] (introduced 1/4/2007)
Cosponsors (1)

864. H.J.RES.4
Every Vote Counts Amendment.
Sponsor: Rep Green, Gene [D, TX-29] (introduced 1/4/2007)
Cosponsors (2)

865. H.J.RES.5
Proposing an amendment to the Constitution of the United States relating to limitations on the amounts of contributions and expenditures that may be made in connection with campaigns for election to public office.
Sponsor: Rep Kaptur, Marcy [D, OH-9] (introduced 1/4/2007)
Cosponsors (1)

866. H.J.RES.6
Proposing an amendment to the Constitution of the United States to provide that Representatives shall be apportioned among the several States according

to their respective numbers, counting the number of persons in each State who are citizens of the United States.
Sponsor: Rep Miller, Candice S. [R, MI-10] (introduced 1/4/2007)
Cosponsors (31)

967. H.J.RES.7
Proposing a balanced budget amendment to the Constitution of the United States.
Sponsor: Rep Musgrave, Marilyn N. [R, CO-4] (introduced 1/4/2007)
Cosponsors (1)

868. H.J.RES.8
Proposing an amendment to the Constitution of the United States to repeal the twenty-second article of amendment, thereby removing the limitation on the number of terms an individual may serve as President.
Sponsor: Rep Serrano, Jose E. [D, NY-16] (introduced 1/4/2007)
Cosponsors (None)

869. H.J.RES.9
Proposing an amendment to the Constitution of the United States authorizing the Congress and the States to prohibit the act of desecration of the flag of the United States and to set criminal penalties for that act.
Sponsor: Rep Emerson, Jo Ann [R, MO-8] (introduced 1/5/2007)
Cosponsors (28)

870. H.J.RES.10
Proposing an amendment to the Constitution to provide for a balanced budget for the United States Government and for greater accountability in the enactment of tax legislation.
Sponsor: Rep Emerson, Jo Ann [R, MO-8] (introduced 1/5/2007)
Cosponsors (None)

871. H.J.RES.11
Proposing an amendment to the Constitution of the United States relating to voluntary school prayer.
Sponsor: Rep Emerson, Jo Ann [R, MO-8] (introduced 1/5/2007)
Cosponsors (1)

872. H.J.RES.12

Proposing an amendment to the Constitution of the United States authorizing the Congress to prohibit the physical desecration of the flag of the United States.

Sponsor: Rep Murtha, John P. [D, PA-12] (introduced 1/11/2007)

Cosponsors (72)

873. H.J.RES.13

Proposing an amendment to the Constitution of the United States relating to school prayer.

Sponsor: Rep Murtha, John P. [D, PA-12] (introduced 1/11/2007)

Cosponsors (None)

874. H.J.RES.16

Proposing an amendment to the Constitution of the United States to repeal the sixteenth article of amendment.

Sponsor: Rep King, Steve [R, IA-5] (introduced 1/17/2007)

Cosponsors (6)

875. H.J.RES.17

Proposing an amendment to the Constitution of the United States establishing English as the official language of the United States.

Sponsor: Rep Doolittle, John T. [R, CA-4] (introduced 1/17/2007)

Cosponsors (None)

876. H.J.RES.19

Proposing an amendment to the Constitution of the United States to establish English as the official language of the United States.

Sponsor: Rep Tancredo, Thomas G. [R, CO-6] (introduced 1/18/2007)

Cosponsors (5)

877. H.J.RES.21

Proposing a balanced budget amendment to the Constitution of the United States.

Sponsor: Rep Buchanan, Vern [R, FL-13] (introduced 1/31/2007)

Cosponsors (6)

878. H.J.RES.22

Proposing an amendment to the Constitution of the United States relating

to marriage.
Sponsor: Rep Lungren, Daniel E. [R, CA-3] (introduced 2/6/2007)
Cosponsors (46)

879. H.J.RES.23
Proposing an amendment the Constitution of the United States relative to abolishing personal income, estate, and gift taxes and prohibiting the United States Government from engaging in business in competition with its citizens.
Sponsor: Rep Paul, Ron [R, TX-14] (introduced 2/7/2007)
Cosponsors (4)

880. H.J.RES.24
Proposing an amendment to the Constitution of the United States to limit the number of consecutive terms that a Member of Congress may serve.
Sponsor: Rep Platts, Todd Russell [R, PA-19] (introduced 2/8/2007)
Cosponsors (None)

881. H.J.RES.28
Proposing an amendment to the Constitution of the United States regarding the right to vote.
Sponsor: Rep Jackson, Jesse L., Jr. [D, IL-2] (introduced 2/13/2007)
Cosponsors (51)

882. H.J.RES.29
Proposing an amendment to the Constitution of the United States regarding the right of all citizens of the United States to a public education of equal high quality.
Sponsor: Rep Jackson, Jesse L., Jr. [D, IL-2] (introduced 2/13/2007)
Cosponsors (None)

883. H.J.RES.30
Proposing an amendment to the Constitution of the United States regarding the right of citizens of the United States to health care of equal high quality.
Sponsor: Rep Jackson, Jesse L., Jr. [D, IL-2] (introduced 2/13/2007)
Cosponsors (3)

884. H.J.RES.31
Proposing an amendment to the Constitution of the United States relating to equality of rights and reproductive rights.

Sponsor: Rep Jackson, Jesse L., Jr. [D, IL-2] (introduced 2/13/2007)
Cosponsors (None)

885. H.J.RES.32
Proposing an amendment to the Constitution of the United States respecting the right to decent, safe, sanitary, and affordable housing.
Sponsor: Rep Jackson, Jesse L., Jr. [D, IL-2] (introduced 2/13/2007)
Cosponsors (None)

886. H.J.RES.33
Proposing an amendment the Constitution of the United States respecting the right to a clean, safe, and sustainable environment.
Sponsor: Rep Jackson, Jesse L., Jr. [D, IL-2] (introduced 2/13/2007)
Cosponsors (None)

887. H.J.RES.34
Proposing an amendment to the Constitution of the United States relative to taxing the people of the United States progressively.
Sponsor: Rep Jackson, Jesse L., Jr. [D, IL-2] (introduced 2/13/2007)
Cosponsors (None)

888. H.J.RES.35
Proposing an amendment to the Constitution of the United States respecting the right to full employment and balanced growth.
Sponsor: Rep Jackson, Jesse L., Jr. [D, IL-2] (introduced 2/13/2007)
Cosponsors (1)

889. H.J.RES.36
Proposing an amendment to the Constitution of the United States to abolish the Electoral College and provide for the direct election of the President and Vice President by the popular vote of all citizens of the United States regardless of place of residence.
Sponsor: Rep Jackson, Jesse L., Jr. [D, IL-2] (introduced 2/13/2007)
Cosponsors (2)

890. H.J.RES.38
Proposing an amendment to the Constitution of the United States to authorize the line item veto.
Sponsor: Rep Platts, Todd Russell [R, PA-19] (introduced 2/27/2007)
Cosponsors (None)

891. H.J.RES.40

Proposing an amendment to the Constitution of the United States relative to equal rights for men and women.

Sponsor: Rep Maloney, Carolyn B. [D, NY-14] (introduced 3/27/2007)

Cosponsors (204)

892. H.J.RES.41

Proposing an amendment to the Constitution of the United States to clarify that the Constitution neither prohibits voluntary prayer nor requires prayer in schools.

Sponsor: Rep Rahall, Nick J., II [D, WV-3] (introduced 3/29/2007)

Cosponsors (None)

893. H.J.RES.45

Proposing a balanced budget amendment to the Constitution of the United States.

Sponsor: Rep Gillibrand, Kirsten E. [D, NY-20] (introduced 6/12/2007)

Cosponsors (32)

894. H.J.RES.46

Proposing an amendment to the Constitution of the United States to deny United States citizenship to individuals born in the United States to parents who are neither United States citizens nor persons who owe permanent allegiance to the United States.

Sponsor: Rep Paul, Ron [R, TX-14] (introduced 6/13/2007)

Cosponsors (7)

895. H.J.RES.48

Proposing an amendment to the Constitution of the United States regarding the requirement of the approval of a two-thirds majority of the Supreme Court for any pardon or reprieve granted by the President.

Sponsor: Rep Cohen, Steve [D, TN-9] (introduced 8/3/2007)

Cosponsors (2)

896. H.J.RES.56

Proposing an amendment to the Constitution of the United States to temporarily fill mass vacancies in the House of Representatives and the Senate and to preserve the right of the people to elect their Representatives and Senators in Congress.

Sponsor: Rep Baird, Brian [D, WA-3] (introduced 10/4/2007)
Cosponsors (1)

897. H.J.RES.57
Proposing an amendment to the Constitution of the United States relating to Congressional succession.
Sponsor: Rep Rohrabacher, Dana [R, CA-46] (introduced 10/4/2007)
Cosponsors (1)

898. H.J.RES.60
Proposing an amendment to the Constitution of the United States providing for Representatives to be chosen every four years, and to limit the number of times Senators and Representatives may be elected.
Sponsor: Rep Goode, Virgil H., Jr. [R, VA-5] (introduced 10/24/2007)
Cosponsors (None)

899. H.J.RES.61
Proposing an amendment to the Constitution of the United States relating to contributions and expenditures intended to affect elections.
Sponsor: Rep Higgins, Brian [D, NY-27] (introduced 10/31/2007)
Cosponsors (1)

900. H.J.RES.63
Proposing an amendment to the Constitution of the United States authorizing the President to disapprove or reduce items of appropriation.
Sponsor: Rep English, Phil [R, PA-3] (introduced 11/13/2007)
Cosponsors (1)

901. H.J.RES.66
Proposing an amendment to the Constitution of the United States to establish and protect the rights of victims of violent crimes.
Sponsor: Rep Chabot, Steve [R, OH-1] (introduced 12/6/2007)
Cosponsors (None)

902. H.J.RES.71
Proposing an amendment to the Constitution of the United States to limit the number of years Representatives and Senators may serve.
Sponsor: Rep Price, Tom [R, GA-6] (introduced 12/18/2007)
Cosponsors (None)

903. H.J.RES.73

Proposing an amendment to the Constitution of the United States relating to the process by which the House of Representatives chooses the President of the United States in the event no candidate receives a majority of the electoral votes.

Sponsor: Rep Sherman, Brad [D, CA-27] (introduced 12/18/2007)

Cosponsors (None)

904. H.J.RES.74

Proposing an amendment to the Constitution of the United States relating to marriage.

Sponsor: Rep Gohmert, Louie [R, TX-1] (introduced 12/19/2007)

Cosponsors (None)

905. H.J.RES.75

Proposing an amendment to the Constitution of the United States relating to the process by which the House of Representatives selects the President in the event no candidate receives a majority of electoral votes.

Sponsor: Rep Goode, Virgil H., Jr. [R, VA-5] (introduced 12/19/2007)

Cosponsors (None)

906. H.J.RES.80

Proposing an amendment to the Constitution of the United States prohibiting the penalty of death.

Sponsor: Rep McCollum, Betty [D, MN-4] (introduced 4/16/2008)

Cosponsors (4)

907. H.J.RES.81

Proposing an amendment to the Constitution of the United States to control spending.

Sponsor: Rep Campbell, John [R, CA-48] (introduced 4/30/2008)

Cosponsors (38)

908. H.J.RES.82

Proposing an amendment to the Constitution of the United States allowing castration after conviction for the rape of a child under 16 years of age.

Sponsor: Rep Broun, Paul C. [R, GA-10] (introduced 5/8/2008)

Cosponsors (None)

909. H.J.RES.83

Proposing an amendment to the Constitution of the United States providing that the Constitution does not preclude a penalty of death, including when it is imposed for the rape of a child under 16 years of age.

Sponsor: Rep Broun, Paul C. [R, GA-10] (introduced 5/8/2008)

Cosponsors (None)

910. H.J.RES.89

Proposing an amendment to the Constitution of the United States relating to marriage.

Sponsor: Rep Broun, Paul C. [R, GA-10] (introduced 5/22/2008)

Cosponsors (91)

911. H.J.RES.96

Proposing an amendment to the Constitution of the United States to permit the penalty of death for the rape of a child.

Sponsor: Rep Chabot, Steve [R, OH-1] (introduced 6/26/2008)

Cosponsors (15)

912. H.J.RES.97

Proposing an amendment to the Constitution of the United States relating to parental rights.

Sponsor: Rep Hoekstra, Peter [R, MI-2] (introduced 6/26/2008)

Cosponsors (None)

913. H.J.RES.98

Proposing an amendment to the Constitution of the United States to limit the number of times Senators and Representatives may be elected.

Sponsor: Rep Kuhl, John R. "Randy", Jr. [R, NY-29] (introduced 9/18/2008)

Cosponsors (None)

914. H.J.RES.99

Proposing an amendment to the Constitution of the United States concerning the election of the Members of the House of Representatives.

Sponsor: Rep Larson, John B. [D, CT-1] (introduced 9/24/2008)

Cosponsors (None)

Senate

915. S.J.RES.1

A joint resolution proposing an amendment to the Constitution of the United States relative to require a balanced budget and protect Social Security surpluses.

Sponsor: Sen Craig, Larry E. [R, ID] (introduced 1/4/2007)

Cosponsors (1)

916. S.J.RES.2

A joint resolution proposing an amendment to the Constitution of the United States relative to limiting the number of terms that a Member of Congress may serve.

Sponsor: Sen Vitter, David [R, LA] (introduced 1/12/2007)

Cosponsors (1)

917. S.J.RES.10

A joint resolution proposing an amendment to the Constitution of the United States relative to equal rights for men and women.

Sponsor: Sen Kennedy, Edward M. [D, MA] (introduced 3/27/2007)

Cosponsors (24)

918. S.J.RES.11

A joint resolution proposing an amendment to the Constitution of the United States to clarify that the Constitution neither prohibits voluntary prayer nor requires prayer in schools.

Sponsor: Sen Byrd, Robert C. [D, WV] (introduced 3/29/2007)

Cosponsors (7)

919. S.J.RES.19

A joint resolution proposing an amendment to the Constitution of the United States relative to Proposing an amendment to the Constitution of the United States which requires (except during time of war and subject to suspension by Congress) that the total amount of money expended by the United States during any fiscal year not exceed the amount of certain revenue received by the United States during such fiscal year and not exceed 20 per centum of the gross national product of the United States during the previous calendar year.

Sponsor: Sen Shelby, Richard C. [R, AL] (introduced 10/1/2007)

Cosponsors (None)

920. S.J.RES.21

A joint resolution proposing an amendment to the Constitution of the United States relating to contributions and expenditures intended to affect elections.

Sponsor: Sen Schumer, Charles E. [D, NY] (introduced 10/18/2007)

Cosponsors (3)

921. S.J.RES.24

A joint resolution proposing a balanced budget amendment to the Constitution of the United States.

Sponsor: Sen Graham, Lindsey [R, SC] (introduced 11/13/2007)

Cosponsors (3)

922. S.J.RES.27

A joint resolution proposing an amendment to the Constitution of the United States relative to the line item veto.

Sponsor: Sen Dole, Elizabeth [R, NC] (introduced 12/11/2007)

Cosponsors (7)

923. S.J.RES.31

A joint resolution proposing an amendment to the Constitution of the United States relating to United States citizenship.

Sponsor: Sen Vitter, David [R, LA] (introduced 4/9/2008)

Cosponsors (None)

924. S.J.RES.39

A joint resolution proposing an amendment to the Constitution of the United States to abolish the electoral college and to provide for the direct popular election of the President and Vice President of the United States.

Sponsor: Sen Nelson, Bill [D, FL] (introduced 6/6/2008)

Cosponsors (None)

925. S.J.RES.40

A joint resolution proposing an amendment to the Constitution of the United States authorizing the Congress and the States to prohibit the act of desecration of the flag of the United States and to set criminal penalties for that act.

Sponsor: Sen Vitter, David [R, LA] (introduced 6/12/2008)

Cosponsors (None)

926. S.J.RES.43

A joint resolution proposing an amendment to the Constitution of the United States relating to marriage.

Sponsor: Sen Wicker, Roger F. [R, MS] (introduced 6/25/2008)

Cosponsors (17)

111th Congress (2009-2010)

House

927. H.J.RES.1
Proposing a balanced budget amendment to the Constitution of the United States.
Sponsor: Rep Goodlatte, Bob [R, VA-6] (introduced 1/6/2009)
Cosponsors (179)

928. H.J.RES.2
Proposing an amendment to the Constitution of the United States regarding presidential election voting rights for residents of all United States territories and commonwealths.
Sponsor: Rep Christensen, Donna M. [D, VI] (introduced 1/6/2009)
Cosponsors (2)

929. H.J.RES.4
Health Protection Amendment of 2009
Sponsor: Rep McCollum, Betty [D, MN-4] (introduced 1/6/2009)
Cosponsors (None)

930. H.J.RES.5
Proposing an amendment to the Constitution of the United States to repeal the twenty-second article of amendment, thereby removing the limitation on the number of terms an individual may serve as President.
Sponsor: Rep Serrano, Jose E. [D, NY-16] (introduced 1/6/2009)
Cosponsors (None)

931. H.J.RES.6
Proposing an amendment to the Constitution of the United States relating to voluntary school prayer.

Sponsor: Rep Emerson, Jo Ann [R, MO-8] (introduced 1/7/2009)
Cosponsors (None)

932. H.J.RES.7
Proposing an amendment to the Constitution to provide for a balanced budget for the United States Government and for greater accountability in the enactment of tax legislation.
Sponsor: Rep Emerson, Jo Ann [R, MO-8] (introduced 1/7/2009)
Cosponsors (None)

933. H.J.RES.8
Proposing an amendment to the Constitution of the United States authorizing the Congress and the States to prohibit the act of desecration of the flag of the United States and to set criminal penalties for that act.
Sponsor: Rep Emerson, Jo Ann [R, MO-8] (introduced 1/7/2009)
Cosponsors (2)

934. H.J.RES.9
Every Vote Counts Amendment
Sponsor: Rep Green, Gene [D, TX-29] (introduced 1/7/2009)
Cosponsors (None)

935. H.J.RES.11
Proposing an amendment to the Constitution of the United States to provide that Representatives shall be apportioned among the several States according to their respective numbers, counting the number of persons in each State who are citizens of the United States.
Sponsor: Rep Miller, Candice S. [R, MI-10] (introduced 1/7/2009)
Cosponsors (28)

936. H.J.RES.13
Proposing an amendment to the Constitution of the United States relating to limitations on the amounts of contributions and expenditures that may be made in connection with campaigns for election to public office.
Sponsor: Rep Kaptur, Marcy [D, OH-9] (introduced 1/8/2009)
Cosponsors (6)

937. H.J.RES.14
Proposing an amendment to the Constitution of the United States to limit

the number of consecutive terms that a Member of Congress may serve.
Sponsor: Rep Platts, Todd Russell [R, PA-19] (introduced 1/8/2009)
Cosponsors (4)

938. H.J.RES.15
Proposing an amendment to the Constitution of the United States to authorize the line item veto.
Sponsor: Rep Platts, Todd Russell [R, PA-19] (introduced 1/8/2009)
Cosponsors (None)

]939. H.J.RES.16
Proposing an amendment to the Constitution of the United States to repeal the sixteenth article of amendment.
Sponsor: Rep King, Steve [R, IA-5] (introduced 1/8/2009)
Cosponsors (1)

940. H.J.RES.21
Proposing an amendment to the Constitution of the United States relative to the election of Senators.
Sponsor: Rep Dreier, David [R, CA-26] (introduced 2/11/2009)
Cosponsors (8)

941. H.J.RES.28
Proposing an amendment to the Constitution of the United States regarding the right to vote.
Sponsor: Rep Jackson, Jesse L., Jr. [D, IL-2] (introduced 3/3/2009)
Cosponsors (None)

942. H.J.RES.29
Proposing an amendment to the Constitution of the United States regarding the right of all citizens of the United States to a public education of equal high quality.
Sponsor: Rep Jackson, Jesse L., Jr. [D, IL-2] (introduced 3/3/2009)
Cosponsors (None)

943 H.J.RES.30
Proposing an amendment to the Constitution of the United States regarding the right of citizens of the United States to health care of equal high quality.

Sponsor: Rep Jackson, Jesse L., Jr. [D, IL-2] (introduced 3/3/2009)
Cosponsors (None)

]944. H.J.RES.31
Proposing an amendment to the Constitution of the United States relating to equality of rights and reproductive rights.
Sponsor: Rep Jackson, Jesse L., Jr. [D, IL-2] (introduced 3/3/2009)
Cosponsors (None)

945. H.J.RES.32
Proposing an amendment to the Constitution of the United States respecting the right to decent, safe, sanitary, and affordable housing.
Sponsor: Rep Jackson, Jesse L., Jr. [D, IL-2] (introduced 3/3/2009)
Cosponsors (None)

946. H.J.RES.33
Proposing an amendment the Constitution of the United States respecting the right to a clean, safe, and sustainable environment.
Sponsor: Rep Jackson, Jesse L., Jr. [D, IL-2] (introduced 3/3/2009)
Cosponsors (None)

]947. H.J.RES.34
Proposing an amendment to the Constitution of the United States relative to taxing the people of the United States progressively.
Sponsor: Rep Jackson, Jesse L., Jr. [D, IL-2] (introduced 3/3/2009)
Cosponsors (None)

948. H.J.RES.35
Proposing an amendment to the Constitution of the United States respecting the right to full employment and balanced growth.
Sponsor: Rep Jackson, Jesse L., Jr. [D, IL-2] (introduced 3/3/2009)
Cosponsors (None)

949. H.J.RES.36
Proposing an amendment to the Constitution of the United States to abolish the Electoral College and provide for the direct election of the President and Vice President by the popular vote of all citizens of the United States regardless of place of residence.

Sponsor: Rep Jackson, Jesse L., Jr. [D, IL-2] (introduced 3/3/2009)
Cosponsors (None)

950. H.J.RES.37
Proposing an amendment to the Constitution of the United States relating to marriage.
Sponsor: Rep Lungren, Daniel E. [R, CA-3] (introduced 3/4/2009)
Cosponsors (41)

951. H.J.RES.41
Proposing an amendment to the Constitution of the United States to prohibit the President from entering into a treaty or other international agreement that would provide for the United States to adopt as legal tender in the United States a currency issued by an entity other than the United States.
Sponsor: Rep Bachmann, Michele [R, MN-6] (introduced 3/25/2009)
Cosponsors (38)

952. H.J.RES.42
Proposing an amendment to the Constitution of the United States relating to parental rights.
Sponsor: Rep Hoekstra, Peter [R, MI-2] (introduced 3/31/2009)
Cosponsors (141)

953. H.J.RES.43
Proposing a balanced budget amendment to the Constitution of the United States.
Sponsor: Rep Buchanan, Vern [R, FL-13] (introduced 4/22/2009)
Cosponsors (1)

954. H.J.RES.47
Proposing an amendment to the Constitution of the United States giving Congress power to prohibit the physical desecration of the flag of the United States.
Sponsor: Rep Emerson, Jo Ann [R, MO-8] (introduced 4/30/2009)
Cosponsors (84)

955. H.J.RES.48
Proposing an amendment to the Constitution of the United States relative to abolishing personal income, estate, and gift taxes and prohibiting the

United States Government from engaging in business in competition with its citizens.
Sponsor: Rep Paul, Ron [R, TX-14] (introduced 4/30/2009)
Cosponsors (2)

956. H.J.RES.49
Proposing an amendment to the Constitution of the United States concerning the election of the Members of the House of Representatives.
Sponsor: Rep Larson, John B. [D, CT-1] (introduced 5/5/2009)
Cosponsors (None)

957. H.J.RES.50
Proposing an amendment to the Constitution of the United States relating to marriage.
Sponsor: Rep Broun, Paul C. [R, GA-10] (introduced 5/7/2009)
Cosponsors (43)

958. H.J.RES.51
Proposing an amendment to the Constitution of the United States to permit the penalty of death for the rape of a child.
Sponsor: Rep Gohmert, Louie [R, TX-1] (introduced 5/7/2009)
Cosponsors (14)

959. H.J.RES.52
Proposing an amendment to the Constitution of the United States to temporarily fill mass vacancies in the House of Representatives and the Senate and to preserve the right of the people to elect their Representatives and Senators in Congress.
Sponsor: Rep Baird, Brian [D, WA-3] (introduced 5/20/2009)
Cosponsors (1)

960. H.J.RES.53
Proposing an amendment to the Constitution of the United States relating to Congressional succession.
Sponsor: Rep Rohrabacher, Dana [R, CA-46] (introduced 5/20/2009)
Cosponsors (1)

961. H.J.RES.57
Preserving Capitalism in America Amendment

Sponsor: Rep Turner, Michael R. [R, OH-3] (introduced 6/23/2009)
Cosponsors (104)

962. H.J.RES.59
Proposing an amendment to the Constitution of the United States to protect the rights of crime victims.
Sponsor: Rep Stupak, Bart [D, MI-1] (introduced 7/9/2009)
Cosponsors (1)

963. H.J.RES.61
Proposing an amendment to the Constitution of the United States relative to equal rights for men and women.
Sponsor: Rep Maloney, Carolyn B. [D, NY-14] (introduced 7/21/2009)
Cosponsors (84)

964. H.J.RES.63
Proposing an amendment to the Constitution of the United States to limit the number of years Representatives and Senators may serve.
Sponsor: Rep Price, Tom [R, GA-6] (introduced 12/14/2009)
Cosponsors (1)

965. H.J.RES.67
Proposing an amendment to the Constitution of the United States to limit the number of consecutive terms that a Member of Congress may serve.
Sponsor: Rep Hall, Ralph M. [R, TX-4] (introduced 1/21/2010)
Cosponsors (2)

966. H.J.RES.68
Proposing an amendment to the Constitution of the United States prohibiting corporations and labor organizations from using operating funds for advertisements in connection with any campaign for election for Federal office.
Sponsor: Rep Boswell, Leonard L. [D, IA-3] (introduced 1/21/2010)
Cosponsors (None)

967. H.J.RES.69
Proposing an amendment to the Constitution of the United States to give citizens of the United States the right to enact and repeal laws by voting on legislation in a national election.

Sponsor: Rep Hoekstra, Peter [R, MI-2] (introduced 1/21/2010)
Cosponsors (None)

968. H.J.RES.70
Proposing an amendment to the Constitution of the United States to give citizens of the United States the right to propose amendments to the Constitution by an initiative process.
Sponsor: Rep Hoekstra, Peter [R, MI-2] (introduced 1/21/2010)
Cosponsors (None)

969. H.J.RES.71
Proposing an amendment to the Constitution of the United States to give citizens of the United States the right to recall elected officials.
Sponsor: Rep Hoekstra, Peter [R, MI-2] (introduced 1/21/2010)
Cosponsors (None)

970. H.J.RES.73
Proposing an amendment to the Constitution of the United States to balance the Federal budget.
Sponsor: Rep Broun, Paul C. [R, GA-10] (introduced 1/27/2010)
Cosponsors (9)

971. H.J.RES.74
Proposing an amendment to the Constitution of the United States permitting Congress and the States to regulate the expenditure of funds by corporations engaging in political speech.
Sponsor: Rep Edwards, Donna F. [D, MD-4] (introduced 2/2/2010)
Cosponsors (26)

972. H.J.RES.75
Proposing an amendment to the Constitution of the United States to balance the Federal budget.
Sponsor: Rep Broun, Paul C. [R, GA-10] (introduced 2/3/2010)
Cosponsors (11)

973. H.J.RES.78
Proposing a balanced budget amendment to the Constitution of the United States.

Sponsor: Rep Bright, Bobby [D, AL-2] (introduced 3/2/2010)
Cosponsors (49)

974. H.J.RES.79
Proposing an amendment to the Constitution of the United States to control spending.
Sponsor: Rep Hensarling, Jeb [R, TX-5] (introduced 3/3/2010)
Cosponsors (53)

975. H.J.RES.82
Proposing the "Doris 'Granny D' Haddock Amendment of 2010" to the Constitution of the United States regarding the authority of Congress and the States to regulate the spending and activities of corporations with regard to political campaigns and campaigns for election for public office.
Sponsor: Rep Hodes, Paul W. [D, NH-2] (introduced 4/14/2010)
Cosponsors (None)

976. H.J.RES.84
Proposing an amendment to the Constitution of the United States giving Congress power to regulate campaign contributions for Federal elections.
Sponsor: Rep Schrader, Kurt [D, OR-5] (introduced 5/13/2010)
Cosponsors (None)

977. H.J.RES.87
Proposing an amendment to the Constitution of the United States. [Requires two-thirds concurrences of both houses of Congress to adopt most changes in internal revenue laws except in certain cases relative to war and national security.]
Sponsor: Rep Neugebauer, Randy [R, TX-19] (introduced 5/26/2010)
Cosponsors (19)

978. H.J.RES.89
Proposing a balanced budget amendment to the Constitution of the United States.
Sponsor: Rep Terry, Lee [R, NE-2] (introduced 6/16/2010)
Cosponsors (None)

979. H.J.RES.95
Proposing an amendment to the Constitution of the United States allowing the States to call a limited convention solely for the purposes of considering

whether to propose a specific amendment to the Constitution.
Sponsor: Rep Minnick, Walter [D, ID-1] (introduced 7/30/2010)
Cosponsors (4)

980. H.J.RES.98
Proposing an amendment to the Constitution of the United States authorizing regulation of any expenditure in connection to an election.
Sponsor: Rep Deutch, Theodore E. [D, FL-19] (introduced 9/29/2010)
Cosponsors (None)

981. H.J. RES. 102
Proposing an Amendment to the Constitution of the United States to give States the right to repeal Federal laws and regulations when ratified by the Legislatures of two thirds of the Several States.
Sponsor: Rep Bishop, Rob [UT-1] (introduced 11/30/2010)
Cosponsors (1)

982. H.J. RES. 106
Proposing an Amendment to the Constitution of the United States relating to the use of foreign law as authority in Federal courts.
Sponsor: Rep Culberson, John Abney (R, TX-7) (introduced 12/22/2010)
Cosponsors (None)

983. H.J. RES. 107
Proposing an amendment to the Constitution of the United States regarding the effect of treties, Executive orders, and agreements with other nations or groups of nations.
Sponsor: Rep Culberson, John Abney (R, TX-7) (introduced 12/22/2010)
Cosponsors (None)

Senate

984 S.J.RES.1

A joint resolution proposing an amendment to the Constitution of the United States relative to limiting the number of terms that a Member of Congress may serve.

Sponsor: Sen Vitter, David [R, LA] (introduced 1/6/2009)

Cosponsors (3)

985. S.J.RES.2

A joint resolution proposing an amendment to the Constitution of the United States authorizing the Congress and the States to prohibit the act of desecration of the flag of the United States and to set criminal penalties for that act.

Sponsor: Sen Vitter, David [R, LA] (introduced 1/6/2009)

Cosponsors (None)

986. S.J.RES.4

A joint resolution proposing an amendment to the Constitution of the United States to abolish the electoral college and to provide for the direct popular election of the President and Vice President of the United States.

Sponsor: Sen Nelson, Bill [D, FL] (introduced 1/8/2009)

Cosponsors (None)

987. S.J.RES.6

A joint resolution proposing an amendment to the Constitution of the United States relating to United States citizenship.

Sponsor: Sen Vitter, David [R, LA] (introduced 1/16/2009)

Cosponsors (None)

988. S.J.RES.7

A joint resolution proposing an amendment to the Constitution of the United States relative to the election of Senators.

Sponsor: Sen Feingold, Russell D. [D, WI] (introduced 1/29/2009)

Cosponsors (3)

989. S.J.RES.11

A joint resolution proposing an amendment to the Constitution of the United

States relative to a seat in the House of Representatives for the District of Columbia.
Sponsor: Sen Murkowski, Lisa [R, AK] (introduced 2/25/2009)
Cosponsors (1)

990. S.J.RES.13
A joint resolution proposing an amendment to the Constitution of the United States relative to parental rights.
Sponsor: Sen Vitter, David [R, LA] (introduced 3/3/2009)
Cosponsors (None)

991. S.J.RES.15
A joint resolution proposing an amendment to the Constitution of the United States authorizing the Congress to prohibit the physical desecration of the flag of the United States.
Sponsor: Sen Vitter, David [R, LA] (introduced 5/6/2009)
Cosponsors (26)

992. S.J.RES.16
A joint resolution proposing an amendment to the Constitution of the United States relative to parental rights.
Sponsor: Sen DeMint, Jim [R, SC] (introduced 5/14/2009)
Cosponsors (6)

993. S.J.RES.20
A joint resolution proposing an amendment to the Constitution of the United States which requires (except during time of war and subject to suspension by Congress) that the total amount of money expended by the United States during any fiscal year not exceed the amount of certain revenue received by the United States during such fiscal year and not exceed 20 per cent of the gross national product of the United States during the previous calendar year.
Sponsor: Sen Shelby, Richard C. [R, AL] (introduced 10/1/2009)
Cosponsors (2)

994. S.J.RES.21
A joint resolution proposing an amendment to the Constitution of the United States relative to limiting the number of terms that a Member of Congress may serve to 3 in the House of Representatives and 2 in the Senate.

Sponsor: Sen DeMint, Jim [R, SC] (introduced 11/10/2009)
Cosponsors (3)

995. S.J.RES.22
A joint resolution proposing an amendment to the Constitution of the United States relative to requiring a balanced budget and granting the President of the United States the power of line-item veto.
Sponsor: Sen LeMieux, George S. [R, FL] (introduced 12/15/2009)
Cosponsors (1)

996. S.J.RES.27
A joint resolution proposing a balanced budget amendment to the Constitution of the United States.

Sponsor: Sen DeMint, Jim [R, SC] (introduced 2/4/2010)
Cosponsors (16)

997. S.J.RES.28
A joint resolution proposing an amendment to the Constitution of the United States relating to contributions and expenditures intended to affect elections.
Sponsor: Sen Dodd, Christopher J. [D, CT] (introduced 2/24/2010)
Cosponsors (3)

998. S.J.RES.35
A joint resolution proposing an amendment to the Constitution of the United States relative to a balanced budget.
Sponsor: Sen Hatch, Orrin G. [R, UT] (introduced 7/21/2010)
Cosponsors (None)

999. S.J.RES.36
A joint resolution proposing an amendment to the Constitution of the United States relative to authorizing regulation of contributions to candidates for State public office and Federal office by corporations and labor organizations, and expenditures by corporate entities and labor organizations in support of, or opposition to such candidates.
Sponsor: Sen Baucus, Max [D, MT] (introduced 7/27/2010)
Cosponsors (None)

1000. S.J.RES.38

A joint resolution proposing a balanced budget amendment to the Constitution of the United States.

Sponsor: Sen DeMint, Jim [R, SC] (introduced 8/3/2010)

Cosponsors (None)

1001. S.J.RES.41

A joint resolution proposing an amendment to the Constitution of the United States relative to equal rights for men and women.

Sponsor: Sen Menendez, Robert [D, NJ] (introduced 12/10/2010)

Cosponsors (7)

Subject Index for 2001-2010

(second part of 102nd-111th Congress)

(Note: The numbers in this index refer to the numbers at the beginning of each entry. These begin where the last volume left off, at number 692.)

Budget,
- Balanced Budget, 695, 696, 698, 714, 724, 761, 776, 786, 793, 806, 831, 837, 846, 849, 853, 860, 862, 867, 870, 877, 893, 907, 915, 919, 922, 927, 932, 953, 970, 972-4, 978. 993, 995-96, 998, 1000
- Putting Certain Trust Funds Outside of, 762

Campaign
- Contributions and Expenditures, 708, 713, 723, 779, 800, 838, 865, 899, 920, 936, 976, 980, 997
- Limiting Corporations and/or Labor Union Advertising & Expenditures, 966, 971, 975, 999

Capital Punishment. See Death Penalty.

Capitalism, Preserving, 961

Castration for Child Rape Conviction, 908, 911

Child Pornography, 706, 752

Citizenship Denied to Those Whose Parents Are Not Citizens, 738, 740, 822, 825, 894, 923, 987

Congress
- House of Representatives
  - Appointments in National Emergencies and Vacancies, 693, 757, 759, 763, 764-65, 767, 783, 809, 826, 851, 896, 959
  - Apportionment Based on Citizenship, 829, 866, 935
  - 4-year Terms, 753, 758, 840, 898, 914, 956
  - Succession of Members (alternates), 809, 897, 960
- Lower Ages for Members from 35 and 30 to 21, 771
- Senate
  - Election to Fill Vacancies, 940, 988
  - Must Approve or Disapprove Nominees Within 120 Days, 756
  - Repeal of Seventeenth Amendment, 788
  - Unanimous Approval to Cut Off Debate, 828

Term Limits, 722, 758, 799, 840, 850, 880, 898, 902, 913, 916, 937, 964-65, 984, 994
Two-thirds Vote Required for Revenue Measures, 977
Also see, Balanced Budget, Spending Limitation, Tax Legislation Limitation or Reform.
Constitutional Amendments
Citizens' Right to Propose, 968
Right to Call Limited Constitutional Convention, 979
Crime Victims, See Victims Rights
Currency, No Treaty Approving Currency Other Than U.S. 951
Death Penalty
Permitted for Child Rape, 909, 958
Prohibition, 906
Desecration of Flag. See Flag Desecration.
District of Columbia, House Seat for, 989
Education, Right to High Quality Public, 728, 811, 845, 882, 942
Electoral College Reform
Change Method by which House of Representatives Selects When No Majority, 775, 903, 905
Direct Election [Sometimes called Every Vote Counts], 769, 774, 796, 804, 818, 827, 854, 864, 889, 924, 924, 949, 986
Votes for Residents of Territories and Commonwealth, 768, 790, 863, 928
Employment (Full) and Balanced Growth, 734, 817, 888
English, Establish as Official Language, 766, 824, 875-76
Environment, Right to, 732, 815, 886, 946
Equal Rights for Men and Women, 735, 781, 819, 852, 891, 917, 963, 1001
Flag, Prevent Physical Desecration, 712, 716, 778, 793, 798, 855, 869, 872, 925, 933, 954, 983, 991
Also see Pledge of Allegiance.
Foreign Law, Restriction on Use of, 982
God, References to, 710, 711, 736, 780, 857
Health, Right to High Quality, 729, 812, 847, 883, 929, 943
House of Representatives. See Congress.
Housing, Right to, 731, 742, 814, 821, 885, 945
Initiative, Citizen Right to Propose Amendments 968
Judges, Reconfirmation of Federal Judges every 10 Years, 720, 747, 833
Life. See Right to Life.Limit Compensation of Public Officials Until General Appropriations are Enacted, 745
Limits on Takings Clause, 832

Line-item Veto. See Veto.
Marriage Definition and/or Protection, 700, 748, 772, 785, 787, 789, 820, 843-44, 848, 856, 878, 904, 910, 926, 950, 957
Martial Law [Congressional Continuity], 851
Non-Natural-Born Citizens Eligible for Presidency or Vice-Presidency after Number of Years, 749, 754, 770, 782, 791, 802, 823
Pardons, Require Two-thirds Approval of Supreme Court, 895
Parental Rights, 912, 952, 988, 990
Pledge of Allegiance, 703, 705, 707, 726, 737. See also, God, References to.
Prayer in Schools, 715, 754, 795, 805, 842, 861, 870, 873, 892, 918, 931
President.
See Electoral College, Non-Natural Born . . ., Pardons, Twenty-second Amendment Repeal, Veto.
Recall, Citizens' Right to Recall Elected Officials, 969
Referendum [Citizen Right to Enact or Repeal Laws], 967
Religious Freedom, 694, 741, 830
Repeal Amendment [Grants Two-thirds of the States Power to Repeal Congressional Legislation], 981
Reproductive Rights, 730, 813, 884, 944
Restoration of Religious Freedom, See Religious Freedom.
Right to Life, 717, 792
School Prayer. See Prayer in Schools.
Seventeenth Amendment (Voters choose U.S. Senators) Repeal, 788
Sixteenth Amendment. See Tax Legislation, Abolition, Amendment, or Reform.
Social Security and/or Insurance, 760, 777, 808, 849, 915
Spending Limitation, 702, 974
Takings Clause. See Limits on Takings Clause.
Tax Legislation
Abolition, Limitation, or Reform, 698, 701, 714, 721, 734, 746, 751, 801, 803, 874, 879, 939, 955. Also see Balanced Budget.
No Taxation Without Representation, 841
Progressive, 733, 816, 887, 947
Term Limits for Congress, 722, 739, 758
Treaties and Executive Agreements, 983
Twenty-second Amendment (Term limits) Repeal, 719, 725, 797, 807, 868, 930
Victims' Rights, 697, 699, 709, 718, 743, 776, 901, 962
Veto, Line-Item, 750, 784, 834-36, 839, 858-59, 890, 900, 932, 938, 994
Voting, Right to, 692, 727, 820, 881, 941

Sponsor Index

(Note: The numbers in this index refer to the numbers at the beginning of each entry. These begin, where the last volume left off, at number 692. Members of the House will have a district number after their states' designations; Senators will not.)

Aderholt, Robert B. (R, AL-4) 832
Akin, W. Todd (R, MO-2) 841
Allard, Wayne (R, CO) 785, 787, 789, 848
Allen, George (R, VA) 860
Andrews, Robert E. (D, NJ-1) 750
Baird, Brian (D, WA-3) 757, 759, 896, 959
Baucus, Max (D, MT) 997
Berry, Marion (D, AR-1) 695, 698
Boswell, Leonard L. (D, IA-3) 966
Broun, Paul C. (R, GA-10) 908-10, 957, 970, 972
Brown, Henry E., Jr. (R, SC-1) 706, 752
Brownback, Sam (R, KS) 856
Bachmann, Michele (R, MN-6) 951
Bright, Bobby (D, AL-2) 973
Buchanan, Vern (R, FL-13) 877, 953
Byrd, Robert C. (D, WV) 861, 918
Campbell, John (R, CA-48) 907
Carter, John R. (R, TX-31) 736
Chabot, Steve (R, OH-1) 699, 743, 901, 911
Christensen, Donna M. (D, VI) 768, 790, 863, 928
Cohen, Steve (D, TN-9) 895
Conyers, John, Jr. (D, MI-14) 754, 791
Cooper, Jim (D, TN-5) 806
Cornyn, John (R, TX) 783, 851
Craig, Larry E. (R, ID) 777, 849, 915
Cunningham, Randy (Duke) (R, CA-50) 712, 798

Culberson, John Abney (R, TX-7)	747, 833, 892, 983
DeMint, Jim (R, SC)	989, 992, 1000
Dingell, John D. (D, MI-15)	713
Dodd, Christopher J. (D, CT)	995
Dole, Elizabeth (R, NC)	784, 859, 932
Doolittle, John R. (R, CA-4)	875
Dreier, David (R, CA-26)	940
Emerson, Jo Ann (R, MO-8)	714, 715, 716, 717, 792-95, 869-71, 931, 932-33, 954
Engel, Eliot S. (D, NY-17)	804
English, Phil (R, PA-3)	771, 900
Feingold, Russell D. (D, WI)	986
Feinstein, Dianne (D, CA)	709, 854
Foley, Mark (R, FL-16)	740, 822
Gillibrand, Kirsten E. (D, NY-20)	893
Gohmert, Louie (R, TX-1)	844, 904, 958
Goode, Virgil H., Jr. (R, VA-5)	766, 898, 905
Goodlatte, Bob (R, VA-6)	862, 927
Graham, Lindsey (R, SC)	921
Green, Gene (D, TX-29)	704, 769, 796, 864, 924
Hall, Ralph M. (R, TX-4)	965
Hatch, Orrin G. (R, UT)	778, 782, 855, 998
Hefley, Joel (R, CO-5)	720
Hensarling, Jeb (R, TX-5)	974
Hoekstra, Peter (R, MI-2)	912, 952, 967-69
Higgins, Brian (D, NY-27)	899
Hodes, Paul W. (D, NH-2)	975
Hollings, Ernest F. (D, SC)	708, 779
Hoyer, Steny H. (D, MD-5)	725, 807
Istook, Ernest J., Jr. (R, OK-5)	694, 696, 724, 830-31
Jackson, Jesse (D. IL-2)	692, 727-34, 773, 810-18, 881-89, 941-49
Jenkins, William L. (R, TN-1)	761, 837
Johnson, Sam (R, TX-3)	751
Kaptur, March (D, OH-9)	838, 865, 936
Kennedy, Edward M. (D, MA)	781, 834, 836, 852, 917
King, Steve (R, IA-5)	803, 874
Kuhl, John R. "Randy", Jr. (R, NY-29)	913
Kyl, John (R, AZ)	776

Landrieu, Mary L. (D, LA)	710, 780, 857
Larson, John B. (D, CT-1)	763, 914, 956
Leach, James A (R, IA-2)	723, 800, 956
LeMieux, George S. (R, FL)	993
Lofgren, Zoe (D, CA-16)	693. 764, 767, 826-27
Lott, Trent (R, MS)	711
Lungren, Daniel E. (R, CA-3)	820, 878, 950
Lucas, Frank D. (R, OK-6)	705, 726
McCotter, Thaddeus G. (R, MI-11)	756
McCullom, Betty (D, MN-4)	847, 906, 929
Maloney, Carolyn B. (D, NY-154)	735, 819, 891, 963
Menendez, Robert (D, NJ)	999
Miller, Candice S. (R, MI-10)	829, 866, 935
Miller, Zell (D, GA)	788
Minnick, Walter (D, ID-1)	979
Murtha, John P. (D, PA-12)	754, 805, 872-73
Michaud, Michael H. (D, ME-2)	760, 808
Murkowski, Lisa (R, AK)	987
Musgrave, Marilyn N. (R, CO-4)	748, 772, 843, 846, 867
Neugebauer, Randy (R, TX-19)	977
Ose, Doug (R, CA-3)	745-46
Owens, Major R. (D, NY-11)	758, 840, 845
Nelson, Bill (D, FL)	924, 986
Pallone, Frank, Jr. (D, NJ-6)	828
Paul, Ron (R, TX-14)	721, 738, 801, 825, 879, 894, 955
Platts, Todd Russell (R, PA-19)	722, 799, 835, 880, 890, 937-38
Pickering, Charles W. "Chip" (R, MS-3)	707, 737
Price, Tom (R, GA-6)	902, 964
Rahall, Nick J, II (D, WV-3)	842, 892
Rangel, Charles B. (D, NY-15)	742, 821
Rohrabacher, Dana (R, CA-46)	765, 770, 802, 809, 897, 960
Royce, Edward R. (R, CA-39)	697
Schrader, Kurt (D, OR-5)	976
Schumer, Charles I. (D, NY)	920
Serrano, Jose E. (D, NY-16)	719, 797, 868, 930
Sessions, Pete (R, TX-5)	701, 718, 734
Shelby, Richard C. (R, AL)	786, 853, 919, 993
Sherman, Brad (D, CA-27)	775, 903
Shows, Ronnie (D, MS-4)	700

Smith, Nick (R, MI-7)	702
Stearns, Cliff (R, FL-6)	839
Stenholm, Charles W (D, TX-17)	753
Snyder, Vic (D, AR-2)	749, 823
Stupak, Bart (D, MI-1)	962
Talent, Jim (R, MO)	858
Tancredo, Thomas G. (R, CO-6)	824, 876
Taylor, Gene (D, MS-4)	762
Terry, Lee (R, NE-2)	978
Turner, Michael R. (R, OH-3)	961
Vitter, David (R, LA-1)	739, 916, 923, 925, 982-83, 987, 990-91
Wicker, Roger F. (R, MS)	926

About the Editor

Dr. John R. Vile (Ph.D., University of Virginia) is a Professor of Political Science and Dean of the University Honors College at Middle Tennessee State University. Vile has written and edited six previous books on the constitutional amending process including the award-winning *Encyclopedia of Constitutional Amendments, Proposed Amendments, and Amending Issues: 1789-2010*, now in its third edition.

Vile is also the author of *Presidential Winners and Losers: Words of Victory and Concession* (2002), *The Constitutional Convention of 1787: A Comprehensive Encyclopedia of America's Founding* (2005), *A Companion to the United States Constitution and Its Amendments*, 5th ed. (2010), and *Essential Supreme Court Decisions: Summaries of Leading Cases in U.S. Constitutional Law*, 15th ed. (2010). He is the editor of *Great American Lawyers: An Encyclopedia* (2001), *Great American Judges: An Encyclopedia* (2003), and a CD-ROM entitled the *History of the American Legal System* (1999).

He is a coeditor of *The Encyclopedia of Civil Liberties in America* (2005), the *Encyclopedia of the First Amendment* (2009), *James Madison: Philosopher, Founder, and Statesman* (2008), and of *Constitutional Law in Contemporary America* (2011). In addition to writing numerous articles and reviews, Vile has authored the introduction for the Lawbook Exchange's 2008 reprint of Noah Webster's *Sketches of American Policy*.

CPSIA information can be obtained at www.ICGtesting.com
Printed in the USA
BVOW04*1130140915

417678BV00004B/14/P

9 781616 191535

